EMOTION AND VIRTUE

A Mental Health Devotional

Brittany Lynn Zuri

Copyright © 2024 Brittany Lynn Zuri

All rights reserved

No part of this book may be reproduced, or stored in a retrieval system, or transmitted in any form or by any means, electronic, mechanical, photocopying, recording, or otherwise, without express written permission of the publisher.

ISBN-13: 979-8-9915143-0-9

Cover design by: Brittany Lynn Zuri

Printed in the United States of America

For my inner child.

*For those who think they are broken and
need to know they are not.*

CONTENTS

Title Page
Copyright
Dedication
Introduction
Shadow Emotions   1
Anger   5
Fear   11
Shame   16
Envy   22
Sadness   27
Light Emotions   33
Joy   36
Peace   41
Love   46
Inspiration   52
Virtues   59

Strength	62
Mercy	68
Honesty	73
Grace	79
Faith	85
Conclusion	90
About The Author	93
Books By This Author	95

INTRODUCTION

First of all, I am not a professional. I have written this book based entirely on my personal experience with mental illness and depression. It is intended to serve as an additional tool for your overall wellness and by no means claims to be a cure or replacement for the soon-to-be-mentioned (or any other available) healing modalities. And of course, I do not recommend changing your health plan without consulting your appropriate doctor.

This book utilizes the principles of cognitive behavioral therapy, or CBT, alongside spiritual practices, Christian influence, and the Dialectical Behavioral Therapy (DBT) understanding of emotions to help you reframe how you see your emotions, mental health, and ultimately yourself. You'll find it structured similarly to a Christian devotional, with Reflections and Activities to help integrate the insights of each chapter.

There are also Spiritual Observations, which help to bring clarity and relevancy to the verses that inspire each chapter. These observations are rooted in my current spiritualist worldview, rather than the Christian upbringing I had. However, while religious trauma is part of my mental health journey, I still find that the word of God can speak to us on a soul level, and outside of the confines of any one religion, it can lead to profound healing and inner understanding. This is why, despite writing this draft more than three years before my spiritual awakening, I decided to keep the verses and the structure that inspired this book. I believe there is no limit to anyone's healing and that however you get there, is the right way for you. Each path is individual and I will not claim that one belief is more valid than another, lest I inflict the same religious trauma I faced onto others.

This book started as a way to collect the verses and affirmations that I had curated for my crystal jewelry business, Violstones, into one document in order to express their importance and practical usefulness on a deeper level than just the crystals themselves. Being a small business owner in the metaphysical community, I often see how people disempower themselves to find all their answers in gemstones. But I strongly believe that crystals, along with other spiritual tools—even affirmations and verses—are tools to point us back to the wisdom that already lives within each of us. With that in mind, I strive to show how the spiritual, the psychological, and the practical can all be integrated into a holistic system of emotional wellness.

Leaning into the idea that our thoughts inspire our feelings—which inspires our beliefs and actions—I hope to offer new thoughts so that we can start to feel differently about ourselves and ultimately believe in our own goodness. Having new ideas for our minds to work with gives us the freedom to choose new actions and live our lives with more joy and hope. My only request for you as the reader, is that you maintain an open mind and commit to the self-exploration that lies before you, whether through this book or on your life path in general. Healing starts with an intention. And in all my years on this mental health journey, I have found that intention is a kind of magic. It can set the course of your life and whether your intentions are good or bad, they have the power to change everything.

So set your intentions with me on this journey. Choose to love yourself, shadows and all, and see yourself well, thriving, and vibrant—the way God and the universe intended for you from the start.

SHADOW EMOTIONS

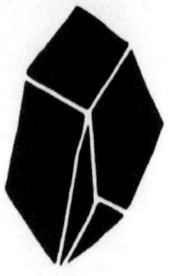

To make friends with your feelings, you must dive into your shadows and hold hands with your bad emotions. But what is the "shadow," and are emotions actually bad? Before we get into the thick of it, let's unpack that.

Shadow work can be seen through two different lenses: by some definitions, shadow work is looking at the socially unacceptable parts of you, the villainous parts, and learning to embrace them. On the other hand, shadow work means delving deep into the subconscious mind and unearthing buried patterns, beliefs, and memories to examine them, and accept or rewrite them. For this book, "shadow work" refers to the latter, and I believe that in understanding the subconscious, we learn to love the scary parts of ourselves, which accomplishes the former.

Now, why go through the effort of uncovering old thought patterns, beliefs, and memories? That is how we make peace with our emotions, especially the difficult ones. This is because thoughts, beliefs, and emotions all work together. The relationship of these three elements is often depicted as a triangle where one influences the other and the other influences another and vice versa.

All three are deeply interrelated. So how you think about something generates how you feel (the emotion) about something, which can color your belief about that thing. For example, unearthing old thought patterns about a childhood memory, allows you to change how you feel about that memory. Similarly, rewriting old beliefs helps to change the way you think so you can, again, feel differently. In this way, shadow work is essential to "taking thoughts captive" and lays the groundwork for true self-acceptance and inner harmony.

Another key thing to understand is that emotions are neutral. They are neither good nor bad. They just are. Emotions are physiological responses to external or internal stimuli. They are natural parts of your human experience and act as signals about the current state of your environment. When life is going well and you feel safe, it generates "good" emotions such as peace, joy, and love. But when you face obstacles, are threatened, or are hurt, you feel "bad" emotions such as anger, fear, or sadness. But those feelings are not bad at all. They are vital to our survival as human beings. According to new studies, psychologists have found that bad feelings are the ones that motivate us to act in the face of adversity.

So as we explore five foundational emotions—anger, fear, shame, envy, and sadness— remember that each of these feelings serves a purpose and are healthy emotions to experience. It's our response to these emotions that make them destructive or not. I invite you to do the shadow work: dive into your sea of "bad emotions." Let yourself be curious about what they are trying to tell you, and refuse to suppress, ignore, or reject them any longer.

ANGER

When we think of bad emotions, anger is usually the first to come to mind. And why not? It's seemingly volatile, aggressive, and explosive. But the truth is anger on its own is none of those things. Our expression of the emotion is what makes it dangerous or not. We can feel anger and choose to breathe through it and set a boundary or we can become combative and throw fists. It's always our choice how we respond to the feelings we experience.

The challenge in our society is that no one has taught us how to express anger safely. We have only ever been told to shut it down and avoid it at all costs. The cost is our health, FYI. Suppressing emotions doesn't make them go away. It only forces the body to store them, leading to physical symptoms like back pain, migraines, stomach aches, and panic attacks. Unfelt emotions are energy that inevitably have to explode at some point, which creates a vicious cycle that fuels the belief that anger and all the other difficult emotions are dangerous. But if we learn to safely and effectively express anger, the explosions don't happen.

The problem is not your anger. Understand that it is an emotion meant to motivate you to overcome obstacles. It's natural to feel angry when someone is standing in the way of your success, when something is not working out how you'd hoped, or when you witness an injustice. These examples produce the natural response of frustration, rage, and bitterness. But what do you do with those feelings? Do you yell, scream, and assault the source? No, definitely not! Anger is a deeply creative and energizing force. You can use it to create solutions, fueling positive change.

A Note on Boundaries

I mentioned before, you can "breathe through it and set boundaries." This idea of setting up barriers has become buzzworthy lately, but let's clarify what healthy boundaries are. Saying you will not tolerate something is not a boundary, but stating your intended consequence for something that crosses you is. Imagine a parent saying, "I will not allow that kind of language in this house!" That doesn't give a clear idea of what to expect if "that language" is used. This kind of statement is a demand that invites someone to do exactly that just to see what happens. But if the parent says, "If you speak to me that way again, you're grounded!" That states a consequence and warns that action will be taken if the boundary is crossed.

Another thing about setting boundaries: don't be

too rigid. Boundaries help us love each other better, not separate us. They are like fences with gates, not moats under brick walls. You allow the people who have earned your trust inside the gate. Like living in a home with a white picket fence, you can stand in your yard and be friendly with neighbors and passersby, but they are not stepping on your lawn without your permission first. Boundaries help us to be kind to ourselves and each other by fostering safety and trust.

Spiritual Observation

Be angry and do not sin. Don't let the sun go down on your anger.

Ephesians 4:26 CSB

In some interpretations, this scripture reads as, "Don't sin by letting anger control you." This can be difficult to understand because it challenges us to do something counterintuitive. Emotions such as anger can feel overwhelming and sometimes seem to arise without us knowing it's happening. So how can we possibly be "letting" it control us if it's out of our control in the first place? Well, that's the lesson here.

Become aware of your emotions. Be an observer of your feelings. Get to know what they look like in you. Once you acknowledge your anger, you must choose how you express it. God believes you are capable, strong, and responsible enough to feel your strong emotions safely. This is why he phrased it in relation to sin (sin, according to Christian belief, is knowing what is right and choosing what is wrong instead). So with that in mind, anger itself is not a sin. But choosing to let emotion dictate your actions in a way that nullifies peace and disgraces harmony is.

This passage reminds us that we are responsible for how we behave and express our feelings. It is our choice and God believes in us to make the right ones. Be angry. Feel the emotion fully, but also learn the skills to move it through your body and heed its message without damaging relationships, property, or yourself.

Reflection and Action

One way to manage anger is called sublimation: using strong emotional energy to create positive changes and impacts in the world. What needs to change in your life? Anger is an indicator of something that isn't working. But instead of destroying what bothers you, how can you set a boundary to keep a relationship healthy or prevent a trigger from activating you again? In what way will you use your emotions to make something beautiful?

Another option for processing anger is to practice physical activity, such as jogging, martial arts, or swimming. This emotion is characterized by sending blood to the limbs, preparing you to fight. So utilize that physical response by engaging in physical activity to help release the energy that's building. This along with acknowledging what you feel, will decrease the intensity and help to clear the mind.

Prayer

I am at peace with my anger. My anger is valid and I know how to feel it safely. I use its force to break down barriers and overcome obstacles. I use it to learn what is important to me and what I want to achieve. My anger fuels evolution. I set boundaries with ease and discernment. I can love others better when I understand my anger instead of suppressing it. Listening to my anger allows me to be in alignment with my needs. Anger gives me a voice to defend myself and others in love.

❋ ❋ ❋

Crystal Recommendations: Carnelian, African Bloodstone, Lava Stone, Tourmaline

FEAR

When we think about mental health, anxiety is one of the most debilitating and most prevalent conditions we face today. According to recent statistics, over 19% of the American population struggles with anxiety of some kind. And that's just in the U.S. At its root, anxiety is an overactive fear response. The emotion of fear is a healthy human reaction that initiates our fight-or-flight response to keep us out of harm's way. When it's healthy, it comes and goes when the perceived dangers are minimized and we feel safe again.

Fear becomes a problem when we don't ever feel safe again. This is when it turns into anxiety and chronic stress, which lead to a plethora of symptoms and emotional distress. It can result in ailments like hypertension, migraines, elevated heart rate, and trouble breathing. So of course, we want to minimize our fears as much as possible.

But fear can be healthy and helpful in our daily lives. Being afraid to walk out into traffic is a definite life-saving effect of healthy fear. Meanwhile, feeling a little anxious before standing in front of an audience can give us the adrenaline boost we need to stay focused and engaged in the presentation. Fear boosts our awareness of our surroundings and energizes us to face our fears. It can be our ally.

This is why healing our nervous system is so important to healing our relationship with fear. An overstimulated nervous system (often the result of compound trauma) can't handle the natural and harmless signals that fear sends. It only becomes more dysregulated, and thus fear becomes overwhelming and debilitating. But when we start soothing the nervous system and bringing it back into balance our fears become more manageable.

A Note on Anxiety and Stress

Some definitions label fear as the emotion of "threat preparation," but what happens when there are no real threats? For those of us fortunate enough to live in first-world countries, the threats we face are minimal. We are not living war-torn, starving, or under threat of fire. So then why do we struggle with such rampant levels of stress and anxiety? While our outside world may appear calm, the internal dialogs that result from capitalism, patriarchy, colonialism, and high-demand religion can be just as traumatic as external oppression. These internal binds result in the same levels of trauma on an emotional level as facing physical or sexual abuse, all of which lead to a massively dysregulated nervous system. As mentioned before, an unbalanced nervous system is more susceptible to unbearable fear, anxiety, and stress.

Spiritual Observation

For God has not given us a spirit of fear, but of power and of love and of a sound mind.

2 Timothy 1:7 NKJV

Two things struck me when I read this verse. One: fear is an option that can be refused because God has given us something better. While fear is one of the involuntary physical responses humans can experience, we can have some control over how much we feed into it. This is an invitation to reconsider how real the threats we respond to are. If we let our minds run away with worst-case scenarios instead of gaining some perspective and grounding ourselves in the facts, we set ourselves up to feel more overwhelmed than we need to. And that's not to invalidate the worries and stressors we face, but it's a call to remember that we are safe and do not need to perceive everything as a life-or-death situation.

Two: how can power, love, and a sound mind be God's prescription for fear? By giving us divine courage and strength we are empowered to defend ourselves and face our worst moments. He reminds us of the innate love planted within us which emboldens us to do what's right despite the consequences. Just like Jesus loved us, despite the coming atrocity of his death. If we choose to act in love we don't need to fear anything as it is the greatest force in the world. Finally, a clear, sound mind with the will to take dark thoughts captive raises our capacity to face and overcome our fears. When we use discernment and discipline our minds to focus on the facts, the good, and the hopeful, we exercise restraint and power over the body, instead of being a victim to it.

Remember, we are not always in danger; we have everything we need to face any threats when we focus our minds and hearts on the divine gifts within.

Reflection and Action

Express gratitude for the gifts God has given you. Believe that you are powerful by reciting affirmations to yourself daily and whenever you face challenging situations. Cultivate a peaceful mind with quiet reflection and journaling. Getting your worries out on paper helps to minimize their urgency. Expand your heart through loving kindness meditations. Focusing on your capacity to show and receive love helps to reduce the mind's focus on fear. Also, focus on regulating your nervous system if you struggle with chronic stress and anxiety. Regular exercise, social connection, an anti-inflammatory diet, and soothing self-care can help restore a healthy balance so fear feels more manageable.

Prayer

I am more powerful than my fear. I claim my god given gifts of love, courage, and a sound mind. I have the clarity to know when a threat is real and when I am overthinking. I can show love in the face of stress. I soothe and comfort myself so my mind and body are balanced. I am safe and I can handle my emotions when they arise. There is nothing to fear. My power is a divine right. My love is a divine right. My mental health is a divine right. I am healthy, stable, and strong. I believe this to be true, now and always.

✹ ✹ ✹

Crystal Recommendations: Labradorite, Howlite, Amethyst, Honey Calcite

SHAME

Shame is one of the emotions that I had trouble accepting as valuable and helpful. Since we now know all emotions serve a purpose, I couldn't help but wonder how shame could benefit me. When we think of shame and the definitions we've come to know, it's the emotion that tells us something is wrong within us, and we must hide ourselves to avoid abandonment. It's a tough emotion to deal with, and so many of us bear the burden of it for the majority of our lives. Whether it was instilled in us through childhood bullying, abuse, or religious dogma, shame can become engrained in the very fabric of our personalities.

The shame that stems from trauma is not the same adaptive, healthy shame that helps us grow. I've learned there are two different kinds of shame that need to be recognized and understood. Healthy shame is the emotion of self-development. We feel it when we see something in ourselves that is out of alignment with who we truly are. This allows us to make necessary changes and be more authentic in the world. Toxic shame is the emotion that reinforces the idea that we are too damaged, we are inherently flawed, and there's nothing we can do to fix it. This is the shame that drives people into crippling depression and suicidality (I know. This was my experience).

The problem is that this kind of shame drives us further away from our true selves. It's born from the ideas, beliefs, and standards of people around us who push them on us via criticisms, rude remarks, and rejections. The message of shame is that there must be something wrong with us. These experiences are so painful that we believe we must mask our true selves so we never feel that pain again.

But in doing that, we lose touch with our souls, feeling more and more disconnected from what makes us sparkle. And deep inside we know something is off and feel ashamed for not being able to do something about it. The vicious cycle eventually leads us to feel nothing at all. And that is a truly dangerous headspace to be in.

We must remember that healthy shame is born from our own thoughts and beliefs, not those of others. This is why connecting with yourself and developing self-compassion is crucial to rewriting toxic shame into healthy shame. When you know and love yourself deeply, you can better assess your outward expression to the world. Were you acting in a way that matches your standards? Were you presenting yourself in a way that aligns with your heart? These are the measurements that matter and that make shame adaptive instead of harmful.

A Note on Shame vs. Guilt

One of the leading researchers on shame, Brene Brown, makes the distinction between shame and guilt very clear. Guilt is the emotion that holds us accountable for our actions. We feel guilty when we've done something wrong. We feel shame when we believe we are bad people. Both emotions drive us to change, but defining ourselves with a label demeans our sense of self-worth. In her book Daring Greatly, Brown calls "for an end to shame as a tool for change." It's better to hold people accountable for their behavior than to imply their character is flawed if you want to see someone grow.

Spiritual Observation

Do not fear, for you will not be put to shame, and do not feel humiliated or ashamed, for you will not be disgraced. For you will forget the shame of your youth, and you will no longer remember the disgrace of your widowhood.

Isaiah 54:4 AMP

This verse is heavy with the promise of God's love and compassion. He will not shame or disgrace us and promises that we will not remember the feelings of humiliation that haunt us because he is not keeping score. The fear of shame can be immobilizing, but this is a promise that we can come to him and he will never shame us for what we say or do. We are welcome in his presence; we are safe with him.

Not only that, but he also reminds us that our world is not defined by what happens to us. In this verse, he is speaking to a woman who has lost her husband, which was the equivalent of social homicide. She was devastated by the prospect of rejection and abandonment from her community. But God speaks directly to that fear when he says she will forget the disgrace of her widowhood. We share in the same comfort as this woman—that no matter what happens to us, our value does not change and we are not subject to the external beliefs of those around us. Only God within us defines our worth.

Reflection and Action

Think back on a time when you first felt ashamed. How has that moment shaped your view of yourself? Go back in your mind to that moment and meet yourself as you were back then. See your inner child and tell them that they are not bad. Shower them with love and nurturing. Hold them in your arms and remind them they are good, no matter what anyone else says. This is called inner child healing and is effective at rewriting old narratives that underline our actions in the present. Also, foster a deeper connection to your true self so that you can define your own standards of living and being.

Prayer

I am a good person. My past does not define me. I live in alignment with my own heart. I release the burden of external expectations. I am confident in my worthiness. I know the difference between shame imposed on me by others and the values I hold for myself. I am guided by my own standards and beliefs about myself. I am inherently good. I am flawless as I am. I am connected to my true self. I define my worth. I live authentically. I share my soul with the world without fear. My authenticity connects me to the right people.

❋ ❋ ❋

Crystal Recommendations: Pyrite, Citrine, Clear Quartz, Petrified Wood, Tiger's Eye

SHAME

ENVY

    Envy tends to get a bad rap in our society (it is considered a deadly sin after all)! But from a psychological standpoint, envy is a normal, healthy, and safe emotion we all have as human beings. Remove the idea of sin for a moment and sit with envy, the emotion. It's here to tell you that you want something; something you don't currently have and that other people seem to have. On a healthy level, this can be motivating and even inspiring. You work out ways to get the thing you don't have. If that's a mate, that can cause you to be more conscious of your presentation and hygiene. If it's a house, it can motivate you to become more resourceful and earn more money. These are healthy by-products of the emotion of envy.
    It becomes problematic when low self-worth, powerlessness, and dishonesty get thrown into the mix. If you don't believe you are worthy enough to go after the thing you see other people have you can find yourself trapped in a vicious loop where you perpetually want what others have but do nothing to satisfy that want. The same

is true if you feel powerless in your life like you can't effectively make positive changes for yourself. Perhaps you choose to obtain the thing you want by dishonest means like stealing or manipulation. That then leads to hurting others and your own integrity as the result of your envy.

But the emotion of envy is not the problem. It's your response to it that can either be healthy or toxic. As with all our emotions, you decide what you do with it.

A Note on Want

Sometimes, wanting things can seem selfish or even sinful, but that's not true. There is nothing wrong with wanting things in life. You are here to experience your life—that means you will desire more than you currently have. These desires motivate us to strive for the best. They inspire us to grow and become more than we ever dreamed. Wants are not harmful or selfish. They are healthy and you are allowed and encouraged to go after them.

Envy vs. Jealousy

These two emotions are often used interchangeably but they are distinct and separate. Jealousy is the emotion that signals to us that something of value is being threatened (e.g., we may lose our significant other to someone else). Envy, on the other hand, arises when we feel we lack something of value for ourselves (e.g., someone else has a significant other that we wish we had). It's a subtle difference, but understanding that difference allows you to receive the messages your emotions are trying to send you so you can respond accordingly.

Spiritual Observation

You should clothe yourselves instead with the beauty that comes from within, the unfading beauty of a gentle and quiet spirit, which is so precious to God.

1 Peter 3:4 NLT

    On the surface, the chosen verse might seem to belittle expressions of beauty that are expressive or loud. But on a deeper level, the verse bypasses all that to say that you are enough exactly as you are. It is a reminder to connect within to your true spirit. Because our souls have no ornaments, clothes, or hairstyles to boast of. In our purest form, we are light—quiet like the universe. We are unfading like starlight. And that is where our true source of beauty and worthiness lies.

    God is asking us to let go of our preoccupation with the external. Forget about what it looks like to other people—whatever IT is. Forget what they look like to you. Tune in to the soul. Tune in to your heart and the heart of others. You may be surprised that they are just as uncertain as you. And that is what unifies us.

We all have enough, but we share the same fear that we don't. When you understand this simple fact—that we are not so separate from each other after all—it becomes easy to quiet down and let go of the need to boast and outperform your fellow human. That gentleness is the beauty that brings us all together.

Reflection and Action

If you feel envy toward someone else, stop and think about how you might attain the object of the envy for yourself. Ask yourself why you want the thing you don't have. Is it because someone somewhere said you need it to fit in and be valuable? Or is it because it brings your soul joy? Learn to know the difference.

If the answer is the latter, make an action plan to achieve the thing you want. What's standing in your way? Do you know you deserve it? Do you know you're allowed to have it too?

Prayer

I am worthy of my desires. I am not being selfish or sinful by wanting things in life. When I see the abundance of other people I let it motivate me to claim that abundance for myself as well. I rejoice in the abundance of others and the emotion of Envy because it shows me the opportunities to grow and expand into my most joyous, generous, resourceful self! I am at peace with my envy and let it come and go freely. I receive its message and use it to the benefit of my highest good and the good of those around me. I heal my relationship with Envy by healing my relationship with my true self. When I know my worth and tune in to my soul's desires, envy is no longer toxic and I am empowered to claim everything I deserve.

❊ ❊ ❊

Crystal Recommendation: Green aventurine, Rose quartz, Pyrite, Blue goldstone

SADNESS

Besides anger, we tend to resist this emotion the most. We feel our eyes well up and our chest caves and we button it up, refusing to let anyone see us cry. But as a society, this resistance to sadness has only led to misunderstanding ourselves and the pain we can experience.

Sadness is the signal that tells us we've lost something important. It is the emotion of loss and shows us that we care deeply. It also is the emotion that connects us to each other. New research has found that when we cry, it stimulates empathy in others and allows us to form deeper bonds. In addition, the physiological benefits of releasing our tears are remarkable. Researchers have also found that crying helps to flush stress hormones and other toxins from the body. This makes sadness an effective emotion for releasing negative energy from the body physically and emotionally.

However, sadness is most often seen as a weakness. So we shut it down and lose the opportunity to connect with our hearts and each other. But when we avoid feeling sad, we risk being complacent with the people and experiences that mean the most to us. Sadness facilitates the growth of our emotional landscape both internally and externally by inviting us to be vulnerable and empathetic. It also allows us to savor the details of our lives and enhances our memory recall. This is partly why it can be so painful—our memories of what we lost become more pronounced. But that doesn't need to be a bad thing. Recounting our memories is part of how we build communities. It's how we honor our ancestors and pass down wisdom.

Sadness is essential to our survival as a society, building relationships and connecting us to our hearts.

A Note on Depression

Depression is most notably characterized by deep sadness. But feeling sad doesn't automatically lead to depression. This misconception is why we tend to avoid the emotion altogether. No one wants to be depressed, especially not when it can lead to critical outcomes such as suicide. But depression is a much more complex mental disorder than simply feeling sad for a prolonged time. Many factors, such as complex trauma, poor diet, genetics, and chronic stress, can influence whether someone will develop a depressive episode or not. However, it should be noted that repressing any emotion, especially sadness or anger, is a sure way to start feeling depressed.

Disconnecting from your feelings only leads to numbness, which is one of the most debilitating symptoms of this condition.

Spiritual Observation

Sorrow is better than laughter, for sadness has a refining influence on us.

Ecclesiastes 7:3 NLT

When I first read this verse, I was struck by the simplicity and profoundness of it. It is jarring to think of sorrow as better than anything (though, the divine did choose its words carefully and didn't say better than joy, just laughter). How could sorrow be better than laughter? Sometimes we get so caught up in distracting ourselves with comedy, games, and parties so we don't have to face our true feelings. But running from our pain and our traumas does not allow us to heal.

All of life is a refinery for human souls. We must burn with sorrow and be tumbled with rough circumstances to come out of this as precious stones. Traumas don't defeat us unless we fail to see how we are being shaped into someone stronger by them. The idea that, "sadness has a refining influence" allowed me to see my pain in a different light, and I hope it strikes you as well. Our pain makes us more valuable, shapes us, and builds us up into our best selves if we are willing to face it, feel it, and grow.

Reflection and Action

Have you been distracting yourself from pain or sadness lately? How can you face it head-on and allow the pain to change you for the better? This emotion nudges us in a more positive direction if we allow it. How can you choose to come through this stronger? What skills will you develop to cope that are empowering and healthy? Will you allow yourself to cry without expectations or judgments, knowing you are growing from this?

Some other ways to process sadness include somatic mindfulness exercises that encourage you to tune into your physical body and identify what your sadness feels like. Name it and the parts of your body that it is affecting. Build trust in yourself so you feel safe enough to let the emotion flow through you and be seen outwardly. Let tears fall and allow yourself to be comforted. Part of the work to make peace with your sadness is to rewrite the narrative that says feeling sad will isolate you. Know that the exact opposite is true.

Prayer

I trust my sadness. My pain gives me valuable information. I tune into my feelings instead of turning away. I allow myself to share my sadness so that my connections grow stronger. Being vulnerable is a strength I possess. Feeling my emotions as they come is good for my mental health. I release any fear preventing me from fully feeling my emotions. I release negativity by expressing my feelings. I allow others to comfort me in my sadness. I allow myself to heal by feeling sad. Feeling loss connects me to what matters in my life. I trust my heart.

❋ ❋ ❋

Crystal Recommendations: Smokey Quartz, Rose Quartz, Black Tourmaline, Amazonite

LIGHT EMOTIONS

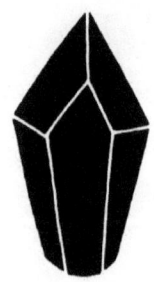

Now that we're familiar with our hard feelings, let's explore the emotions we all crave. In the next few chapters, we'll learn about peace, joy, inspiration, and love. But why are these feelings so crucial to improving our mental health? This is the last piece of the puzzle given what we now know about our thoughts, beliefs, and emotions. Just as thoughts and beliefs can determine how we feel, our emotions can also influence how we think and what we believe. Cultivating peace can influence you to see an experience as less stressful and reinforce the belief that you can handle tough situations. And choosing to find joy in the moment can alter your beliefs about an event from being a disaster to a triumph.

While our shadow emotions help us survive life, cultivating light emotions allows us to enjoy it. But, this must be noted, it does take effort to feel these positive emotions. This is because of a negativity bias, defined as our adaptive focus on the negative in our lives to survive in a dangerous world. But since those of us in first-world countries live in a relatively safe world now, a negative bias is actually maladaptive for most of us. It forces us to hyper-fixate on what's going wrong when we are safe and catastrophize when things are going well.

Another reason this may be difficult to overcome is trauma. Trauma is when an event overwhelms our nervous system past the point of being able to recover and return to a state of calm. When we've faced traumatic experiences in life, that affects our ability to feel safe, and if the trauma is not processed it lives in our bodies. When this happens, our survival mechanisms are constantly activated, making it nearly impossible to focus on the positive. It only makes sense, as it's our body's natural way of trying to survive a threat and keep us safe.

However, the only way to reset the nervous system after it has been traumatized is to feel positive emotions, which are signals that the body is safe and there is no immediate danger. This is why actively cultivating positive emotions is a life-changing habit. So as we dive into the next four emotions, remember that these require an active choice to be felt. But the effort is well worth it if you want to heal your mind and body from the inside out.

JOY

According to most definitions, the emotion of joy is the expression of pleasure with one's experience. Paul R. Rasmussen, Ph.D. even described it as a "celebration of existence." We feel joy when life feels good, fun, and exhilarating. That is the natural physiological response in our body to signal that life is safe and enjoyable.

Like all our emotions, it can happen involuntarily as a natural response to positive experiences. But this emotion can also be cultivated to generate more of itself even when life isn't feeling very positive. Since our brains are naturally wired to highlight the negative going on around us as a way to survive, we sometimes have to actively choose to feel joy even if the external stimuli don't warrant the feeling for us. This choice is how we rewire the synapses to focus on the good and generate a more positive outlook, hopeful disposition, and happier life.

Yes, joy is an emotion. But it is also—and more importantly—a choice that can radically change your overall perspective and mood. Science shows that when we actively focus on feeling good, we lower our stress hormones, boost our immune system, and increase our longevity. Joy is a life-giving emotion! No wonder we all hunt for it so diligently. But we must remember that the power to experience more joy lies within each of us, regardless of our external circumstances.

A Note on Toxic Positivity

I know that claiming that you can experience joy during a tough situation opens the door to what has now been identified as toxic positivity, which is a term psychologists use to describe invalidating someone's real pain and hard experience. Choosing joy should not be a means to bypass difficult feelings, such as sadness or anger about a situation. Rather, the benefits of choosing happiness come when all other options have already been explored. If expressing your anger and working to overcome the obstacle it resulted from is not a feasible option anymore, then choosing to be content amid difficulty would be the best option for preserving your own inner harmony. But to bypass the anger and say you're happy when you're not is only self-betrayal.

Spiritual Observation

Our hearts ache, but we always have joy. We are poor, but we give spiritual riches to others. We own nothing, and yet we have everything.

2 Corinthians 6:10 NLT

When we think of joy, the idea of permanence seems to tag along behind it—this secret hope that joy will never fade or change. But this verse reminds us that joy does not result from perpetual ease in life. Joy is a choice. Despite the pain and suffering we all inevitably experience, God reminds us that joy is a resource that is always available. You can feel sorrow while still holding on to hope and have limitations while still having so much to give. Your smile is like a lighthouse shining in someone's stormy sea. Your laughter is a healing salve for someone's loneliness.

When we tap into our joy, the challenges we face become more meaningful and, as a result, more bearable. Yet, sometimes it can be hard to believe that joy can be found when we face so much turmoil. But that is just the thing—God calls us to release the expectation that joy comes from outside experiences, people, or places. Our joy is cultivated from within, actively chosen to be felt.

In that regard, joy is permanent. We fulfill the hope that it will never fade by our choice. Gratitude for all you have makes space for happiness in the face of lack. And that joy gives more space for more gratitude. This cycle of thankfulness can be contagious if you let it. Acknowledge the pain of life but also acknowledge the blessings. You are allowed to feel grateful, hopeful, and even joyful in the midst of pain. Despair is not the only acceptable response to struggle. Spread joy and gratitude and see how the world and the people around you grow.

Reflection and Action

Some ways you can boost your sense of joy are to practice gratitude daily, explore something new, and practice visualization with happy memories. When you practice gratitude, you train your brain to focus on the good around you more often than the bad. Meanwhile, cultivating "play" time through hobbies or sports allows you to be childlike, without the pressure to do it right, earn money, or keep track of your time. That carefree feeling is one of the best parts of feeling joyful. Lastly, remembering your best memories is an easy hack for your mind and body to savor and internalize the sensation of joy so that it can be easily recalled as needed.

Prayer

I choose joy even when things are not going my way. My joyfulness does not invalidate my experience but honors my sense of well-being. I find joy within and always have access to it whenever I need it. Happiness is one of my greatest resources and I use it freely. I choose to enjoy my life. Anything that does not bring me joy, I know I can change it at any time. My joy is a window into my best features. When I express joy I am most like myself and I allow others to see me in my fullest glory. Joy is my source of abundance, vibrancy, and hope. I choose to feel joyful so that others around me may also feel and spread it worldwide.

❊ ❊ ❊

Crystal Recommendation: Citrine, Aura Quartz, Strawberry Quartz, and Rainbow Moonstone

PEACE

Peace is one of those feelings that blurs the line between emotion and state of mind. Some people would say that peace is an experience and not an emotion. This is because it is something that we most often think of as cultivated and derived from other emotions such as contentment or relaxation. But peace has also been defined as a feeling of calm and well-being, indicating that something is safe and well cared for. It is marked by physiological changes in the body like all other emotional states. When we feel peaceful, blood pressure drops, tension releases from the body, and our mind quiets.

With all the known benefits of feeling peaceful, it makes sense that it's such a highly sought-after state of being. But the whole challenge with peace is that it also is not outside the body. We don't find peace by ingesting food or consuming content. Yes, some herbs reduce anxiety and physically alter our system to allow for more calm, and there are soothing books out there (like this one!) that can influence a new train of thought and create space for more peaceful thoughts to flourish. But, lasting inner peace is an inside job.

We don't experience peace, we feel it. The experience of peace can be produced by outside forces and is short-lived. But when we feel peace as an emotion, it is generated within us. Self-generated peace reinforces itself, allowing us to trust our innate ability to feel at ease regardless of the circumstances. We self-generate the emotion of peace through our thoughts and choices. Much like choosing joy is our responsibility, if we want to feel calm in the storm, we must decide that we will feel peaceful in it. Making that choice empowers us to overcome any challenge with confidence and grace.

A Note on Mindfulness and Mediation

One of the most accessible ways to experience peace is through meditation. If the practice of meditation is new to you, here are some things to keep in mind: meditation is not associated or restricted to any one religion or ideology; a meditation practice can take on many different forms; and you do not have to practice for very long to reap the benefits. Meditating for as little as 3 minutes at a time is a great place to start training your mind to step back from its busy thoughts. The moment you detach from the thoughts is when you give yourself the space to make choices. And that, in my opinion, is the greatest value of mindfulness—giving yourself the option to think/feel/choose differently.

Spiritual Observation

I am leaving you with a gift—peace of mind and heart. And the peace I give is a gift the world cannot give. So don't be troubled or afraid.

John 14:27 NLT

Reflecting on the verse above, Jesus himself said those words. He who embodies God in totality gives us peace. It is through his existence that we see what inner peace looks like in human form. However, I don't think he means that he is the only source; rather, through his example we know how to find peace within ourselves.

Jesus faced just as much persecution and torment as anyone, being harassed, misjudged, betrayed, and ultimately crucified for his beliefs. If anyone knows what stress is, I would say he sure did. But somehow he managed to go down in history as the perfect man. He led with love, healed thousands, and lived authentically, never giving up his truth. Where did that kind of resiliency come from? His sense of inner peace—a knowing that everything will work out as it should.

Jesus rejected fear and doubt in his life. He lived in complete faith and trust in his path. So even the struggles he faced were seen as valuable steps on his journey. That is the result and benefit of inner peace. The gift he left was the power of this simple truth. If he could live this way, so can we.

The world likes to spread fear, worry, and stress and offers peace through things you can buy and consume. It's a very profitable system that keeps us stuck and easy to control. But the reality is, there is nothing to fear and the peace you are seeking is already inside you.

So when you are feeling overwhelmed, remember that Jesus believes in you. He knows you have everything you need. He simply asks us to tap into what already lives within us.

Reflection and Action

As mentioned previously, mediation is a great way to cultivate more inner peace by allowing you to detach from your thoughts and observe them rather than being consumed by them. Also, inner peace comes from releasing judgment. When you choose to accept things as they are, rather than deem them as good or bad, this also detaches you from the outcome of external experiences. Focusing on your own experience with life, instead of the experience of others (and judging if they're doing it "right" or "wrong") allows you to relax and find more contentment with the world around you. Because when you start to look within and feel more of your own good feelings, there will be less to worry about.

Prayer

    I am peaceful by nature. I know exactly how to access the peace that dwells within me. I know I am not my thoughts. I can choose what I think about and how I perceive things to grow more calm in my life. I accept myself and others exactly as they are. This acceptance makes space for harmony in all areas of my life. I live in harmonious bliss with the events in my life. I understand that even difficult situations are vital to my journey and I welcome them gracefully. I relish the fact that peacefulness is my natural state of being. I trust myself and know that I am safe.

❋ ❋ ❋

Crystal Recommendations: Blue Lace Agate, Lapis Lazuli, Amethyst, Blue Calcite

LOVE

Something we all strive for in life is to find and experience love, often at any cost. We want to know that someone cares about us, which helps us validate our inherent worth. But this pursuit is usually external and we place a lot of weight on the love we can get from other people. However, like peace, love is not only a lived experience but also a critical emotional state that needs to be felt and internalized.

The emotion of love is characterized by pleasurable physical reactions in the body such as warmth, euphoria, and heightened energy. It also is known that the power of love changes our lives on a molecular level. In a water memory experiment conducted by Dr. Masaru Emoto, we learned that when water received loving messages it created beautiful ice crystal formations, as opposed to the water receiving hateful messages, which formed disorganized and misshapen crystals instead. The experiment proved that our intentions have the power to change the physical world, defining the patterns of growth we see around us. The lesson here is that since we are also made of water, we can grow into beautiful humans when we feel loved.

Love is one of the strongest forces in the world. No wonder self-love is so transformative. When we turn the love we feel towards romantic partners, friends, or even our pets, on ourselves that can heal deep wounds. When we feel unloved we settle for less than what we want and less than we deserve. But loving yourself means you have your best interests at heart, treat yourself well, and spend time with yourself enjoying your own vibe.

It can be hard to show yourself love when you don't feel it very often in the first place. This is why choosing to feel the emotion of love is so important. Allow yourself to feel the flutter in your stomach when someone compliments you, or the warmth in your chest when a loved one brings you a meaningful gift. Feeling the physical sensations in your body will help you memorize love so you can recreate that emotion within yourself. Make your own stomach flutter and your own chest radiate warm fuzzy feelings.

A Note on People Pleasing

We can think we are loving when we are generous with our time, resources, and effort to make others happy. But there is a risk of people pleasing if the motivations for these behaviors are not genuine. If you are extending a loving hand to someone in need, it must come from a place of genuine care and willingness. People pleasing is motivated by fear, not caring. We say "yes" when we mean "no" and over-extend ourselves to avoid losing connection. That fear of lost connection makes the action that should be loving feel conditional and strained, rather than soul-filling and authentic. Real love is unconditional and grows from trust and safety, not fear and control.

Spiritual Observation

For God so loved the world that he gave his one and only Son, that whoever believes in him shall not perish but have eternal life.

John 3:16 NIV

Regardless of what you believe, this verse is talking about more than salvation. This verse is about sacrificial love. When you think of someone who loves you, you may think along the superficial lines: They think you're cute and find you attractive. You might think deeper: They value you for your personality, respect your needs, and look out for your best interests. But let's go even deeper than that.

Can you fathom being loved so much that someone would die for you? Maybe your parents would. Maybe your spouse. But this love is rare and it's so special. If you feel like no one in your life would, I want you to consider that there is a person in history whose sole mission was just this. He died for you before he even knew you. Think about this: someone loved humanity, with all of its chaos and flaws, pain and horror—he loved it so much, that he died for it.

Now, whether you believe that this person was the son of God or not, that act still took place and that intention was carried through with you in mind. So, just to be clear, you're worth someone's life. You, with all the things you may hate about yourself, you with your hang-ups and your tragedy, you with your alternative ideas and beliefs—you are special. You are worthy of the greatest act of love. You are worth someone's greatest sacrifice.

Reflection and Action

If you internalize that you are so treasured and precious that someone would sacrifice everything for you, how would your self-image change? What would you do to honor that new self-image? To honor how valuable you are? And to take it further, can you imagine turning that love on yourself? What are you willing to sacrifice to show yourself how much you matter?

One way to experience more love is to practice loving kindness meditations. Visualize sending love to everyone including strangers, enemies, and ultimately yourself. You can also do volunteer work which allows you to embody sacrificial love. Finally, you could also try this simple activity: write the words "I AM" in the middle of a blank page. Your mission is to fill in the rest of the page with every positive trait you can think of about yourself to solidify on paper your worthiness.

Prayer

I am worthy of deep, unconditional love. I am precious. I am priceless. I know my worth. I trust that the love I feel from others is genuine. I give the same kind of love I want to receive. I sacrifice all thoughts, beliefs, and behaviors that prevent me from loving myself fully. I accept love from the world easily. I release any doubts about my worthiness. I extend love to myself as much, if not more, as I give love to others. I hold unconditional space for myself. I attract the kind of life I deserve when I love the way God loves me.

Crystal Recommendations: Rose Quartz, Opalite, Ruby, Jade

INSPIRATION

People often say "Follow your dreams!" It's a great notion, but why? It is plastered all over wall art and in ads everywhere. Why is following our dreams so important? Many researchers have found that feeling inspired and motivated is essential to our mental health. And going after our goals is what helps to fuel these feelings.

The emotion of inspiration can be felt as a light bulb moment or a stroke of genius. It helps us to believe in the end outcome, overlooking any limitations. It is transcendent, lifting us to tune into our divine power and capabilities. It empowers us to act and to achieve our wildest dreams. Think about when you've felt inspired. It opens you up to all the possible options and fires up your heart and brain. Without inspiration, we're listless and often hopeless because of the lack of options at our disposal. Having choices is one of the crucial factors to a healthy mind and an optimistic outlook.

Inspiration is the emotion that motivates us to bring our dreams into reality. It creates a desire to manifest something from nothing. According to researcher T.M. Thrash, we can be inspired by something—such as seeing a beautiful dress—which sparks a new idea for how to dress. Or we can be inspired to create something that exhibits some intrinsic value, such as a profound work of art. However we experience it, inspiration is the emotion we need to feel to see new pathways for caring for ourselves and those around us. When we are inspired we become better role models for those around us so that others may feel inspired also. Whenever we see someone taking care of themselves, that can spark an idea for a new habit to try. That spark is sometimes all we need to turn our lives around. So don't be afraid to chase what inspires you. It's your body's natural way of helping you reach new heights.

A Note on Habits vs. Goals

Sometimes these two can get confused. A goal is measurable with an endpoint. Habits are ongoing. That confusion can be why New Year's resolutions fall flat. A good habit can help you reach a goal. A goal can help you develop a healthy habit, such as writing 500 words a day to achieve the goal of publishing a novel. But what do both of these have in common? They need consistent effort to stick. Habits and goals train us to work at something even when we lose the initial spark of inspiration. They help us develop discipline, one of the difficult truths of self-care. Sometimes you must do things even when you don't feel like it. That grit is what builds resilience and self-reliance.

A Note on Manifesting

Manifesting has become a trending topic since the popular book The Secret was released. And with the help of media, we've collectively come to believe that manifesting is instant gratification. But in actuality, manifesting is the result of many different factors aligning to produce a desired outcome. This alignment can take a long time, especially if things are far from the end vision. Manifesting takes effort and work. Whether that's mental and emotional work to align your beliefs and thoughts to the life you want, or physically working to set and achieve small goals to reach the endgame, manifesting can be life-changing but it takes commitment and work to generate what you desire most in life.

Spiritual Observation

All hard work brings a profit, but mere talk leads only to poverty.

Proverbs 14:23 NIV

The Psalms are known for their deep wisdom, so we can trust that it is good advice to work for what matters instead of simply talking about it. Sometimes we can get in the habit of telling people our hopes and dreams as a way to speak them into existence. But that's more of that instant gratification that we believe manifesting to be. God reminds us that we cannot bring anything to life just by talking about it. We must till the earth, plant the seeds, and nurture the sprouts until the harvest.

He is asking us not to shy away from the work that needs to be done, as "All hard work brings a profit." Our efforts are never wasted; we aren't wasting time by putting in the work. Sometimes we get worried that we'll run out of time if we take the long way to our dreams. We feel urgency about accomplishing our goals. So we try quick fixes and shortcuts. But God asks us to trust that it will amount to the abundance we desire. Don't be afraid to struggle along the way or to take more time getting there. It will all be rewarded.

Reflection and Action

Is there a dream you've talked about pursuing but haven't taken solid moves toward yet? What's holding you back? What small action can you do today to bring you closer to your dreams? Will you commit to working for your dreams?

To boost inspiration spend time cultivating happiness and joy. Feeling more positive promotes optimism, which opens up a world of possibilities. Brainstorm ideas and solutions and get in the habit of thinking outside the box. Allow yourself to entertain the ideas that seem impossible. Get to know your limitlessness. Soon you'll know nothing is impossible. Also, practice goal setting by making a game plan for a goal you have. Break it down into small actionable steps. Aim to take action daily if possible. Finally, seek out inspiration in music, nature, and art. Let new ideas come to you from unexpected sources.

Prayer

I am capable of creating my dream life. I follow my inspiration wholeheartedly. I find inspiration everywhere I look. I lean into my optimism and hope. I am limitless. Nothing is standing in my way. I release all doubt and fear. I create the life I want with ease. I am committed to doing the work in my life. My aligned efforts produce much abundance. I am an inspiration to the people in my life. Together we create the future we desire.

❊ ❊ ❊

Crystal Recommendations: Blue Goldstone, Citrine, Fluorite, Labradorite

INSPIRATION

VIRTUES

Positive emotions and virtues go hand in hand, as living virtuously begets positive emotions, and generating positive emotions helps us tune into higher virtues universally recognized to enhance our well-being and quality of life. They are not restricted to any belief but are accepted by all cultures as valuable character traits. Virtues allow us to live within our values, show up authentically, and spread goodness to the world.

Plenty of evidence shows that living a virtuous life is good for your mental health. Similar to the way gratitude rewires the brain for a more positive experience, living with integrity boosts our self-esteem and sense of happiness. Studies suggest this is because focusing on something greater than ourselves connects us to the divine within and outside of us. This connection helps us feel secure in life and leads to more hopefulness.

In this book, I have pinpointed five virtues that I believe when cultivated with intention boost our mental health and renew the mind. They are often considered biblical virtues, but they are, in fact, universal and not limited to the Christian faith. Instilling these values into our daily lives enriches our human experience so that we can love more deeply, feel more peaceful, ignite inspiration in ourselves and others, and enjoy life fully.

STRENGTH

As a society, we have come to think that strength comes from independence. We tend to believe that if we can carry everything ourselves we have accomplished everything in life. Not needing to rely on anyone else is a badge of honor. But where has that led us? To burnout, loneliness, and hopelessness. When we refuse to accept our own limitations we are not being strong; we are making ourselves weaker by literally compromising our immune systems and wearing ourselves down to the point of exhaustion.

So, if shouldering the weight of the world isn't real strength, what is? According to psychologists, inner strength is a combination of positive feelings, like those discussed in this book, and skills such as emotional intelligence, self-compassion, resilience, and distress tolerance. When we practice these skills regularly, we develop a reliable inner strength that is not contingent on external circumstances. This virtue must be cultivated intentionally to grow into a stable force in our lives.

Particularly, the skill of self-compassion gives us room to embrace our weaknesses so that we don't overexert ourselves. We can only be our strongest when we know how much weight is too much. A bodybuilder builds muscle by slowly increasing the payload, not by ignoring their current limitations. Additionally, teamwork researchers have found that we perform better when we are supported and can delegate tasks based on skillsets and expertise. No one needs to face life alone. We are all built for connection and collaboration. Great cities were built by great tribes, not solitary individuals.

A Note on Dissociation

Another way strength can be misrepresented is through dissociation, a state of being where we are distant from the world, our bodies, and reality. This coping mechanism can be subtle and long-standing if we don't regularly tune in to our bodies and emotions. A lot of the time we can find ourselves perpetually daydreaming, feeling numb or disinterested, and lacking a sense of connection to the world around us. As a society, we've grown to accept this state as normal. Unless it becomes a hindrance to our daily lives such as in the case of dissociative disorders, dissociation often goes under the radar because it allows us to deal with more without complaint.

But the reality of dissociation is that it is part of our

stress response. It is activated when we are too stressed and don't have a means of physical escape; instead, we escape mentally by dissociating. The thing to remember here is that it's a stress response. Sure, you can do more and handle the pressure, but you're cutting yourself off from life when you're so stressed you have to disconnect from the world around you to cope. That's not strength. That's pushing yourself past your limits.

Spiritual Observation

Each time he said, 'My grace is all you need. My power works best in weakness.' So now I am glad to boast about my weaknesses, so that the power of Christ can work through me.

2 Corinthians 12:9 NLT

When I first read this verse it changed my life. It reset my perspective on my mental illness. Up until that point I had seen my depression as a flaw, a genetic defect, a cruel curse, and a life sentence. I had never considered it an opportunity for anything. But reading the words of Jesus, "My strength works best in weakness," flipped all of that on its head. My depression was bringing me to my knees so that the divine source of all strength could step in and carry me to the next chapter. I suddenly realized the pressure to fix myself and be strong when I felt so depleted wasn't even my responsibility to bear. This allowed me to sit with my feelings in a way I hadn't before. I didn't have to fight them because that wasn't my job.

I developed strength by not fighting the depression. Because in not fighting it or demonizing it, it suddenly lost its power. And in the battle with mental illness that's half of the struggle: it seems bigger and more powerful than you. And the more you wrestle with it the stronger it gets. But this verse is a reminder that the battle isn't yours. The Holy Spirit can fight it; It is strong enough. All you have to do is admit that you need the help. Admit when you are not strong enough because his divine power works best in your weakness.

Reflection and Action

Think of a struggle you've been facing. Have you been going it alone and pushing yourself to exhaustion, helplessness, and hopelessness? How can you ask for help? Remember you are strongest when you accept what's too difficult for you. Will you promise to listen to your limits and weaknesses and not shame yourself for them? See them as opportunities for the divine to work and shine through you.

Some ways to develop your inner strength include mindfulness practices and nurturing the skills mentioned earlier. Mindfulness allows you to act from the present instead of the past or future. The point of greatest power is in the here and now. If you act from a place of worry about the future or shame about the past then you are robbing yourself of the strength you have to face any situation with confidence and grace. Speaking of grace, cultivating other positive virtues and qualities such as gratitude, inner peace, self-regulation, emotional awareness, and radical acceptance will help you anchor into your own resiliency. Strength training doesn't just apply to physical muscles. To be mentally and emotionally strong, you must also learn and practice the skills that build you up.

Prayer

I am resilient. I am Strong. My strength comes from accepting my own weaknesses. I respect my current limitations. I know when to ask for help. I allow myself to share the load with the people I trust. I do not have to handle everything on my own. I am strongest when I accept support. I am strongest when I trust myself and others. I ask for help without shame or fear. I am brave enough to be authentic and vulnerable. I am confident despite my weaknesses. I grow my inner strength consistently and with ease. When I am authentically strong I connect to those around me and engage in the world more deeply.

Emotions born from this Virtue: peace, love, security

❊ ❊ ❊

Crystal Recommendations: Hematite, Lava Stone, Clear Quartz, Amazonite

MERCY

According to the Netflix show, Cobra Kai, which showcases a "No Mercy!" attitude, sometimes mercy can be confused with weakness. Instead of dealing out punishment and justice, mercy asks us to spare our offenders. But as we learned in the previous chapter, sometimes being strong means that we hold back. When we think of great human rights and civil change leaders, they didn't make their impact by being forceful or ruthless. "An eye for an eye makes the whole world blind," according to Mahatma Gandhi.

Cultivating mercy in our lives means we embody compassion and gentleness in a world that is harsh and devastating all on its own. Think about how many people suffer each day and how many of us face silent battles that no one will ever see. Because of this, mercy is vital to making the world safer, softer, and kinder. We all have to live on this planet and share this experience, and Lord knows we've each seen our share of horror and heartbreak. Showing mercy on each other helps lighten the load.

But what about justice and boundaries and discipline? Mercy doesn't say that we shouldn't pursue justice for wrongdoings. Rather, it is an expression of divine power. When we are in a position of authority and have the power to harm someone else or inflict punishment on them, that is the opportunity to show mercy. And being merciful doesn't only benefit the person on the receiving end; research shows that mercy and compassion boost our sense of well-being, lower our stress, and improve our mental health. You increase your own positive experience with the world, instilling a stronger self-esteem and hope for a kinder planet. In this way, mercy can be contagious. If you can choose kindness over retribution, you inspire others to do the same.

A Note on Forgiveness

Forgiveness is one of those things people struggle with because it feels like letting their enemy off the hook. But that's not what forgiveness is. When we forgive, we aren't forgetting what happened or excusing it and saying it's acceptable. Forgiveness is an internal choice that allows us to feel peace despite the transgressions we've endured. It's for our benefit—no one else's. This act of self-care is vital to your healing and inner peace. Showing mercy and forgiveness when someone has mistreated you is the greatest sign of resiliency and maturity. It takes a deeply compassionate heart to hold space for yourself while also saying, "I'm not holding this against you and I can move on with my life despite the hurt you've caused me. Be well and be at peace." Set your boundaries and walk away if you need to, but forgive them because your mental health and happiness depend on it.

Spiritual Observation

Blessed are the merciful, for they will be shown mercy.

Matthew 5:7 NIV

When I think about this relative to mental health and hardship, one of the common prayers in these situations is "Have mercy on me!" The pain feels too intense and it feels like it will last forever. So we ask God, and even beg, for mercy, for some relief. But then what is also common is our lack of mercy for others, especially those who harmed us and caused this pain in the first place.

Jesus is challenging us to do a hard thing with this verse. It's a reminder of forgiveness and kindness because he knows what good it can do for our hearts. The mercy we so desperately need for relief from the pain of past hurts starts within you and your willingness to let go of grudges, hatred, and ill will toward others. Once you begin to show mercy to others, forgive them like God forgave us, the pain you feel can heal and the prayer for mercy on your suffering is finally answered.

Reflection and Action

Is there a situation you are facing right now that feels overwhelming that you need mercy for? Can you think of anyone you are blaming for your situation? How can you be more merciful rather than bitter and harsh despite your trials? Instead of asking for mercy in your situation, try asking Spirit to grant you the chance to be merciful.

Ways to cultivate more mercy include volunteering and fostering patience in your daily life. Volunteer work is the perfect example of being in a position of power and using that power to benefit others instead of harming them. Fostering patience and kindness allows you to see the flaws in people around you without judging them. Reducing judgments will also help mercy come more naturally as it will show you that no one is perfect.

Prayer

I am understanding. I am kind. I am gentle. I feel empathy for my fellow human beings. I release all judgments that keep me from being kind. I release the expectations that keep me from being gentle. I show mercy to all who cross my path. I reclaim my power by choosing kindness over retribution. I choose forgiveness for my own well-being. I experience more peace when I forgive. I empower others to be more loving when I show mercy first. I change the world around me when I am kind.

Emotions born from this virtue: love, peace, hope, confidence

* * *

Crystal Recommendations: Amazonite, Rhodonite, Turquoise, Rose Quartz

HONESTY

When we think of being honest, we imagine confessions and telling the truth before a judge. But honesty is more about vulnerability with ourselves than it is about outward expressions of truth. As a virtue, opening up with others has its benefits, such as stronger relationships, more trust, and deeper empathy for each other. However many of us forget that to create open and honest relationships with others, we first need to be honest with ourselves.

This is where that shadow work comes in. We have to be willing to look at ourselves and the emotions we try to hide, the memories we don't want to remember, and understand our personal experiences on a much deeper level. What are our motivations? What are we truly afraid of? Answering those questions helps us to heal so that we are no longer dictated by what hurt us. That kind of healing only comes when we are willing to look at the wound in the first place.

Vulnerability is a challenging trait to develop as it

is in direct opposition to our survival mechanisms. Fear helps keep us safe, remember? So when we try to open up, we're often faced with our own blocks: what if I'm rejected? What if I'm too much? What if I'm not enough? So to avoid the risk we hide ourselves and can even lie to ensure our connection with the people around us. But this masking, and essentially dishonest representation of the self only keeps us more disconnected.

Cultivating honesty within allows us to show up authentically with others. Being authentic means that people can trust what you say and do because it is coming from your true feelings. When we say and act out of alignment with how we truly feel that causes friction not only with the people around us but also internally. Being dishonest with ourselves worsens our mental health as it reduces our sense of inner peace and joy while also breeding shame. Honesty allows us to share our true feelings, set healthy boundaries, and align with the right people. Feeling truly seen happens when we "see" ourselves.

This is how we overcome our fears of being rejected, isolated, and disconnected. These fears are natural parts of being human and help to keep us safe. We are tribal beings who thrive in communities. So it makes sense that to be a part of the collective we tend to hide our truth to feel secure and belong somewhere. But the trade-off for being seen should never be your authenticity.

A Note on Emotional Safety

The challenge of being authentic is that we will face rejection. That is the inevitable part of being honest in the world. And for many of us rejection can be a source of trauma. So to keep our nervous systems happy we avoid that trauma at all costs. But the issue with that is if you never show up with your honest truth, you'll never find the people who are safe for you. Learn to discern who makes you feel emotionally safe and who doesn't. This discernment is healthy and allows you to keep your boundaries with those who are not for you and to open up with those who are supportive.

Spiritual Observation

And don't say anything you don't mean. This counsel is embedded deep in our traditions. You only make things worse when you lay down a smoke screen of pious talk, saying, 'I'll pray for you,' and never doing it, or saying, 'God be with you,' and not meaning it. You don't make your words true by embellishing them with religious lace. In making your speech sound more religious, it becomes less true. Just say 'yes' and 'no.' When you manipulate words to get your own way, you go wrong.

Matthew 5:37 MSG

In this passage, Jesus draws our attention to an old covenant and law put in place before his death on the cross: Say what you mean, and don't lie. He knows that we like to embellish our words to appease other's expectations. We like to bet on the future and make promises. But Jesus is reminding us that we have no control over anything other than our own actions in the present moment.

How many times have you said you can do something for someone, promised a certain outcome, only to have everything work against you so that you fail to meet the expectation you promised? Or vice versa. Someone promised you something and let you down? I know for me it's been too many times to count. And it hurts. It leads to a disheartened mistrust in humanity. Which only fosters us to keep our hearts hidden and our authenticity shrouded.

But Jesus is asking us to not trust in humanity, but rather trust ourselves and keep it simple. Say yes if you mean yes and no if you mean no. Because when you're honest with yourself and others you can show up in the world at your best. We shine the brightest when we feel safe and seen.

Reflection and Action

How can you keep it simple? Have you promised someone something outside of your limits? Can you be honest and admit this to them and to yourself? How can you set boundaries with yourself and others that align with your true feelings? As a challenge: Will you say what you mean and mean what you say in one moment today?

One way to cultivate more openness and vulnerability in your relationships is by boosting your emotional intelligence. Create a habit of checking in with your emotional state with the help of apps like How We Feel. Learning to identify how you feel will help you recognize when you are perhaps acting out of alignment with your truth. Also, work on overcoming people-pleasing behaviors and recognizing when you are hiding yourself to make others happy.

Prayer

I am open. I am honest with myself. I am safe to be vulnerable. I am safe to be authentic. I share my true self with others. I shine brightest when I am authentic. Vulnerability is a strength. Honesty comes easily to me. I create deeper relationships by being honest. I build trust through vulnerability. I trust myself to say what I mean and mean what I say. I own the power of my words. I choose to speak my truth

Emotions born from this Virtue: peace, trust, love, confidence

❉ ❉ ❉

Crystal Recommendations: Clear Quartz, Black Tourmaline, Selenite, Citrine

GRACE

After all the talk we've had about love and mercy, it begs the question: what is grace? On the surface, they all seem so much alike that it can be hard to see their individual value. We've explored love as an emotion that signals to us that our relationships are safe. We've looked at mercy and its propensity to illicit compassion and forgiveness. And in all of that, there is grace, which is the ability to accept the flaws of others and ourselves and show love and mercy regardless. In a psychological sense, grace is how we welcome others into our lives. When we hold space for others as they share their authentic selves, that is grace in action. When we advocate for others and demand inclusivity, that is grace— unconditional love— for each other.

In religious texts, the concept of salvation hangs on grace and God's willingness to show us love despite our imperfections. Specifically in the Christian faith, grace seems to imply unworthiness or inherent badness. According to most interpretations, it is given as a gift to someone who doesn't deserve it. But as I've come to understand it, grace and unconditional love are not gifts from God to people who are unworthy of love. It's a gift from ourselves to ourselves because we believe we are sinful. Giving ourselves grace means we accept who we are, flaws, trauma, issues, and all— the same way that God inherently loves us. God doesn't see us as bad or unworthy. We do and we've created entire religions around this idea of our brokenness. But that's not how God sees us, and his unconditional love and untainted view of us is Grace in its greatest expression.

A Note on Perfectionism

The underlying beauty of grace is that despite imperfection, we are loved and accepted by a higher power. But somehow, that knowledge doesn't seem to allay the desire to be perfect for many of us. Perfectionism is described by psychologists as an overly critical self-evaluation and exceedingly high standards. According to the research, this drive to produce flawless results in life has been linked to depression, anxiety, suicide, and even physical health issues like high blood pressure, Crohn's disease, and cardiovascular disease. Toxic perfectionism truly is dangerous to both our physical and emotional well-being.

The whole point of grace is to help us combat that drive, by giving us the space to make mistakes and produce less-than-perfect outcomes without the fear of rejection or punishment. However, like all the other emotions and traits that can cause us problems, perfectionism serves a function. It helps us guarantee our acceptance and the praise of our peers. That validation helps us feel secure in our place in the world. Grace offers us that validation without the need to be perfect.

Spiritual Observation

But God showed his great love for us by sending Christ to die for us while we were still sinners.

Romans 5:8 NLT

Knowing what I know now, the last phrase "while we were still sinners," strikes me as harsh. It feels like a pitiful outlook on humanity. But the key to remember is that sinner is a term of damnation, not unworthiness. Being a sinner doesn't mean you are unlovable, cast out, or rejected. In fact, as a sinner, you were loved with such great sacrificial love that the creator of all things sent down the dearest part of himself to die for you! You didn't have to earn that. He did that for you of his own choosing. It's the kind of love that chooses you despite your quirks, hang-ups, mistakes, or bad habits.

If I'm being honest, it's a love I don't fully understand sometimes. But it's real. While you are struggling, while you are hurting, while you disgrace yourself, while you hurt others, while you choose to indulge in bad habits despite knowing the consequences—through all of that God loves you so much that he chose to suffer and die like any other human. He died for your soul and future. And that's the thing about grace: you didn't have to change yourself to deserve that. Before you were even born, just as you are now, scars and all, including future mistakes, God's promise still stands. You are lovable and worthy. You never have to earn validation or belonging. You are accepted always and forever.

Reflection and Action

With the idea of grace and unearned unconditional love in mind, is there something you feel you fall short in and maybe hold against yourself? When you hear the word "sinner" do you imagine the worst part of yourself and others? And does that perception of yourself sometimes justify your negative self-talk or judgment? Can you write down these "worst traits" and physically cross them out, visualizing that Jesus did just that when he died on the cross? Try to let go of the need to earn love. Imagine who you are with the security of grace as part of your identity. How will that empower you to overcome toxic perfectionism?

Some ways to overcome perfectionism and cultivate more acceptance include mindfulness practices such as yoga, and loving-kindness meditation. Yoga is a good way to tune into your body and understand your limitations on a physical level and extend grace to those limitations by accepting them and working with them rather than pushing yourself to the point of self-injury. Also, loving kindness mediations as mentioned before help to foster gentleness toward yourself and others even when they feel difficult to love.

Prayer

I am worthy. I accept myself. I belong here just as I am. I am loved just as I am. I do not need to earn love. My value is not dependent on my perfection. My imperfections do not disqualify me. I show myself the same grace that God has for me. I have always been loved and always will be. I am capable of unconditional love. I choose to accept others even when they are difficult to love. I release the need for perfection from myself and others. Grace allows me to show up as I am without shame. When I extend grace to others I allow others to know the validation and safety of divine love.

Emotions born from this Virtue: love, joy, hope

✢ ✢ ✢

Crystal Recommendations: Aura Quartz, Rainbow

Moonstone, Rose Quartz, Opalite

FAITH

According to the dictionary, faith is the "complete trust or confidence in someone or something without proof." Trust in the unknown helps us function without thinking about it. We have faith that our cars will function every morning, that our food is safe, and that our eyes will open tomorrow. If we didn't have faith in those mundane things we'd be paralyzed by fear and never do anything at all. Faith is essential to overcoming anxiety and fear. It allows us to trust what we can't be certain of when a lack of certainty is at the core of the human experience.

Faith as a virtue means building trust in the forces outside of our control. This has been linked to lower stress levels and a greater sense of peace and contentment. Cultivating faith benefits not only your spiritual health but also your physical and mental health as well. Researchers all over the world can vouch for the healing effects of spirituality and faith in unseen forces. But perhaps the greatest benefit of faith would be the capacity to trust in yourself when you don't have proof that you will overcome the challenges you face. This is the gift that allows all the other virtues to take root and flourish. If you didn't trust in your own resiliency, inner peace, or joy, then the healing impact of cultivating those qualities would be less notable. It's because of our faith that we believe we can heal and grow in the first place.

A Note on the Placebo Effect

Some might resist the idea of faith and call it a placebo effect, which is defined as the positive result of a dummy treatment that has no therapeutic properties. However, the belief that it will have a positive effect seems to manifest the results regardless. While doctors might dismiss this and say that the results of such an effect are void, I believe this is the perfect example of the power of faith. Without any proof that a treatment will work, the belief that it will is what generates enough hope and power to determine the desired outcome. That is what faith can do in our daily lives. If we trust in the unseen forces at work we can bring about the changes we want to see, simply by believing that the changes can and will happen.

A Note on Religious vs. Spiritual Faith

Even though we have spent this book working with Christian Bible verses and examined these virtues through a religious lens, it must be said that there is a difference between religion and spirituality. While a religion follows a distinct set of laws and practices, spirituality is more individual and intuitive. Both afford us access to higher powers and allow us to tap into faith, but each functions differently. Neither is right or wrong. They are simply options that bring us closer to divinity. And as we've discussed, that is the purpose of virtues. They connect us to the divine within, to our highest expression of self so that we can bring more goodness into the world.

Spiritual Observation

So we do not focus on what is seen, but on what is unseen. For what is seen is temporary, but what is unseen is eternal.

2 Corinthians 4:18 CSB

This verse is like the biblical version of the phrase I've heard so often in the mental health world: "This too shall pass." Everything around us is temporary, our houses, our money, our health, our pain—none of it lasts forever. We can waste so much of our already limited time worrying and feeling depressed about things that are limited. The key to breaking the cycle of mental illness is choosing to focus on something else. You have to choose to acknowledge that your struggles are not eternal and that there are things we can't see at play.

This verse highlights a promise. It is asking us to

trust in our future. Believe that after the struggle there will be peace and rest. That intentional belief is what shapes the outcome. Our faith is a powerful manifesting force and it is the catalyst for change and healing. Instead of focusing on what is right in front of you and the limitations that seem to surround you, God reminds us that there is a whole universe of alternatives, possibilities, and chances available to us. The future is only limited by what we believe is possible. So choose to believe in your own happiness. Have faith in the unlikely outcomes, the heavenly paradise, and the hope of your destiny.

Reflection and Action

Consider the struggles you are facing right now. Do you feel like they will last forever? Can you choose to believe in another possible outcome? Can you trust in the promise that this too shall pass?

Ways to cultivate more trust and spiritual faith include prayer and being in nature. Connecting to the divine through prayer allows you to actively trust in a force outside of yourself and stimulate a sense of faith in the unseen and unknown. Similarly being in nature connects us to the spirit of the earth and the interconnectedness of all things. Standing at the beach with the horizon before you can remind you how big the world is and give a bit of perspective to the struggles you may be facing.

Prayer

I trust in the unseen. I am guided by faith. I am safe to trust in the bigger picture. I release control and fear. I surrender to the process. I trust myself. I have faith in my own power and strength. I trust my inner wisdom. I listen to my intuition. My faith is on my side. The divine is working in my favor.

Emotions born from this Virtue: peace, hope, gratitude

※ ※ ※

Crystal Recommendations: Amethyst, Labradorite, Fluorite, Celestite

CONCLUSION

After taking this journey through these fourteen Emotions and Virtues, I hope you begin to see how your feelings are not your enemies. We gain more from life by listening to our emotions and learning their language. And we can transform our daily lives through the virtues that instill a sense of self-trust and remind us that we are actually good at heart.

There has been so much programming in our society that we tend to believe that we are naturally bad and so are our emotions. But I hope that through this book you realize the opposite is true. We are not inherently bad with a need to be cleansed and purged of negativity. We are inherently good and only need to reconnect with our inner selves to find this is true. There is nothing wrong with feeling anger, fear, or sadness. These negative emotions guide us to understand ourselves, our environment, and the world so that we can live more authentically.

My prayer as you carry on your journey is that you will fall deeply in love with all of you, that you will find peace in your emotional world, and that your mind will feel safe again. I hope after going through this series you've learned these core foundations: Emotions are not the problem, you have the power to choose the life you want and how you feel about it, and every moment is a choice. Will you choose to listen to how you feel or will you continue to ignore your body's natural signals to what feels good and what doesn't? Or will you choose to believe in your divine right to wellness? Will you choose to see yourself as God sees you?

I affirm that we are all sacred beings and that there is no quota on what you need to believe in order to heal. God never meant for the gateway to your health and happiness to be a narrow doorway. Religion can make it seem that way sometimes. But I hope that this book has helped to open your mind to the possibility that God is bigger than any one belief and that your well-being is truly all that matters. God left us message after message and promise after promise to remind us that our health is not only critical to the enjoyment of the human experience, it's also completely within our reach.

Recovery from trauma can be difficult and daunting; and by no means do I aim to discredit the hardships we all face by implying that any of this work is easy. But I want to reiterate that we all have a part to play, a responsibility, in our journey and how we heal or don't. Your relationship with your emotions, yourself, and your mind determines if you find the peace and joy you are looking for. Trust me, I know from experience that resisting and fighting yourself and how you truly feel only prolongs the suffering. So, with the help of this devotional, I hope you begin to choose self-acceptance, compassion, and understanding more and more.

Our thoughts are like habits in our minds; to break bad habits (like self-sabotage and negative self-talk), you must replace them with new healthier habits. This book hopefully showed you your thought habits and the areas of work you have left to do. But I also pray that this book provided replacement thoughts for you to begin making new choices for your daily life. Through intentionally slowing down and tuning into our souls, our feelings, and our natural right to health in every regard, we find that our healing is inevitable.

ABOUT THE AUTHOR

Brittany Lynn Zuri

Brittany Lynn Zuri is a mental health advocate and small business owner with a B.A. in Creative Writing. Blending all her passion and skills, her business, Violstones, uses crystals, wearable art, and affirmations to heal her community. Follow and support her journey at www.violstones.com and on Instagram at @Violstones.

BOOKS BY THIS AUTHOR

The Power Of Intention Affirmation Deck

Coming Winter 2024

Find peace and clarity with intuitively painted affirmation cards channeled to offer guidance for any mood or circumstance. Remember you always have the power to choose your path; you are the creator of your reality through the power of your intentions and thoughts.

Follow me on Instagram at @violstones to pre-order your deck today and come along for the behind-the-scenes production process.

www.ingramcontent.com/pod-product-compliance
Lightning Source LLC
Chambersburg PA
CBHW071234090426
42736CB00014B/3083